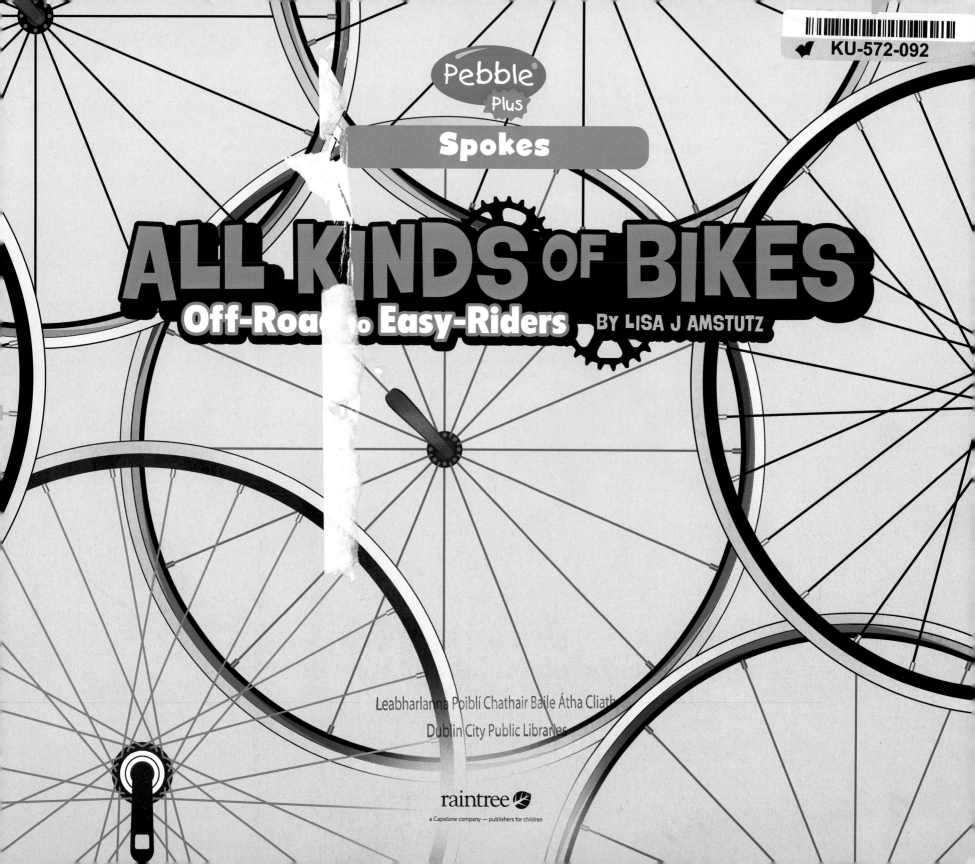

Pebble®
Plus

Spokes

ALL KINDS OF BIKES
Off-Road to Easy-Riders
BY LISA J AMSTUTZ

raintree
a Capstone company — publishers for children

Raintree is an imprint of Capstone Global Library Limited, a company incorporated in England and Wales having its registered office at 264 Banbury Road, Oxford, OX2 7DY – Registered company number: 6695582

www.raintree.co.uk
myorders@raintree.co.uk

Edited by Jeni Wittrock
Designed by Kyle Grenz
Production by Jennifer Walker
Picture research by Sarah Schuette
Photo Schedule by Marcy Morin
Production by Capstone Global Library Ltd
Printed and bound in India.

ISBN 978 1 4747 3372 4 (hardback)
20 19 18 17 16
10 9 8 7 6 5 4 3 2 1

ISBN 978 1 4747 3377 9 (paperback)
21 20 19 18 17
10 9 8 7 6 5 4 3 2 1

British Library Cataloguing in Publication Data
A full catalogue record for this book is available from the British Library.

Acknowledgements
We would like to thank the following for permission to reproduce photographs: Alamy: Tim sport, 9; Dreamstime: Carlos Santos, 17, Juriah Mosin, 21; Getty Images: Stone/Andre Gallant, 5, Taxi/Jordan Siemens, 7, Workbook Stock/ Mark A Johnson, 13; Glow Images: Cusp/Corbis/Steve Prezant, 19; iStockphotos: AnastasiyaShanhina, 11; Newscom: Image Broker/Jim West, cover; Shutterstock: Jacek Chabraszewski, 15

Design Elements
Shutterstock: filip robert, Kalmatsuy Tatyana

We would like to thank Gail Saunders-Smith for her invaluable help in the preparation of this book.

Every effort has been made to contact copyright holders of material reproduced in this book. Any omissions will be rectified in subsequent printings if notice is given to the publisher.

All the internet addresses (URLs) given in this book were valid at the time of going to press. However, due to the dynamic nature of the internet, some addresses may have changed, or sites may have changed or ceased to exist since publication. While the author and publisher regret any inconvenience this may cause readers, no responsibility for any such changes can be accepted by either the author or the publisher.

Contents

Let's go!

Some bikers love to race. Others cruise off the paved path. Some riders do daring stunts. For every kind of rider, there is a bike to match.

City bikes

Road bikes are perfect
for short trips around town.
Thin tyres zip over streets.
Riders switch gears to make
it easy to pedal uphill.

Track bikes are light
and fast. Riders race
them on indoor tracks.
Disc wheels slice through
the air for more speed.

Take your time

Touring bikes are made for long bike trips. Their frames are light but strong. They can carry water bottles and bags.

Riders sit low to the ground on recumbent bikes. These bikes are comfortable for long rides. Riders lean back in their seats.

No roads

Not all bikes need roads or tracks. A mountain bike travels in the countryside. The bike's wide, bumpy tyres grip rough trails.

BMX bikes fly over tracks
with ramps. These bikes have
stunt pegs. While doing
tricks, riders can stand
on the pegs or the pedals.

peg ⊢━━━┫

EASTPAK®

EASTPAK® U.S.A.

ibis HOTEL

Even more bikes

Not all bikes have two wheels.

Bikers with good balance can

ride one-wheeled unicycles.

Tricycles have three wheels.

They are hard to tip.

Want to cycle with friends?

A multibike seats three

or more people. Or take one

friend on a tandem bike.

It is built for two!

Glossary

balance ability to stay steady and not fall over

disc wheel light but solid wheel for a bike; disc wheels help indoor racers go faster

gear round, toothed part of a bike that turns the tyres; different gears make it easier to push a bike's pedals

grip hang on tight

pave cover with a hard surface such as cement or tar

recumbent bike comfortable kind of bicycle that is built to allow the rider to lean back in the seat

stunt trick that shows great skill or daring

stunt peg tube attached to the wheel of a BMX bike; the rider can stand on the peg or balance it on a ledge

Read more

BMX (Cool Sports), Aaron Carr (AV2, 2012)

Mountain Biking (Exploring the Outdoors), Michael De Medeiros (AV2, 2013)

Race That Bike: Forces in Vehicles (Feel the Force), Angela Royston (Raintree, 2016)

Websites

www.cyclesprog.co.uk/get-cycling/tour-de-france-kids-guide
Find out all about the famous cycling race, the Tour de France.

www.dkfindout.com/uk/sports/cycling
Discover lots of facts about bikes and cycling on the DK Find Out! website.

Index